V. Long

# HERTFORD'S PAST
# IN PICTURES

**Also by Len Green**

Hertford Green Coat School and the Newton Exhibition Foundation
(Hertford and Ware Local History Society Occasional Paper, No. 1 — 1989)

The Cowper Testimonial School, Hertford
(Hertford and Ware Local History Society Occasional Paper, No. 3 — 1992)

# HERTFORD'S PAST
# IN PICTURES

by

Len Green

*To Vera and Peter*

*Len Green*

The Rockingham Press

First published 1993
by The Rockingham Press
11 Musley Lane,
Ware, Herts SG12 7EN

**A catalogue record for this book is available
from the British Library**

**ISBN 1 873468 17 2**

Printed in Great Britain by
Biddles Limited
Guildford

**Part of the proceeds of this book are donated to
the Hertford Museum**

# Contents

Acknowledgements   6

Introduction   7

A Tour of the Town:

    Fore Street and Parliament Square   8

    The Wash, the Castle and Old Cross   18

    Maidenhead Street to South Street   26

    Northwards: Cowbridge to Bengeo   34

    Westwards: St. Andrew Street to Hertingfordbury   41

    Southwards: the London Road to Church Street   48

    Eastwards: Ware Road   52

    Gascoyne Way: a Mixed Blessing   55

Courts, Alleys and Yards   62

Big Houses   68

Rivers and Mills   74

Railways   84

Malting, Brewing and Inns   88

The Place of Work   100

Shops and Shopkeepers   110

Churches   122

Going to School   128

Notable Occasions   140

Sports, Pastimes and Entertainment   148

Hertford's cinemas   154

In Time of War   156

Hertford People   161

Index   167

# Acknowledgements

I must express my thanks to the many people who have shown interest in this project, especially to those whose memories go back further than the sixty years I have spent in Hertford. Some of them were boys in the classes I taught when I came in 1933 and in the few years before I came big changes had taken place in the town.

I must also acknowledge the many people who have lent me photographs for this book and, in mentioning their names, I apologise if I have left anyone out: Mrs. E. Bird, Ann Bridges, Margaret Brown, Baden Browne, Mrs. D.L. Chaplin, David Dent, Jean Gilby, Mrs. S.M. Gillett, Phyl Halls, Mrs. Iley, Bruce Johnson, F. McEwen, Brian Maling, Dr. G.W. May, Sylvia Mear, Rosemary Mnich, Mrs. J. Neal, Mrs. W. North, Mary Ollis, Mrs. Pateman, Charles Toghill and Leslie Welch. I also acknowledge with thanks the great help and loan of photographs received from Addis Ltd., Stephen Austin and Sons Ltd., Ekins & Co Ltd. and McMullen and Son Ltd., with particular thanks to their museum curator, Mr. Stan Springett. Other photographs are from my own collection, from the Elsden Collection which is owned by the Hertford Camera Club and from the collection of the late E.S. Etheridge.

I am also grateful to the Royal Commission on the Historical Monuments of England for permission to use their Copyright photographs on pages 68, 70 and 71, all from the National Buildings Record. I am indebted to the staff of the Hertford Record Office for their generous help in answering my questions. Finally, I must thank the Hertford Museum and particularly Andrea George, Rosemary Bennett and Margaret Harris, for all their unstinting help and advice and for the loan of photographs from the Museum's extensive collections.

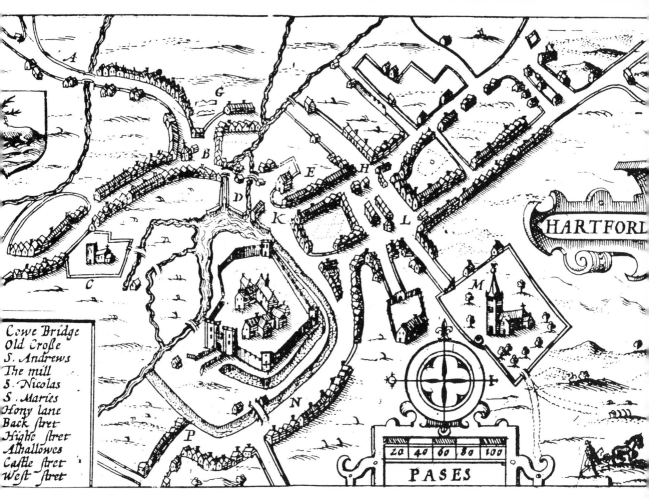

Cowe Bridge
Old Croſſe
S. Andrews
The mill
S. Nicolas
S. Maries
Hony lane
Back ſtret
Highe ſtret
Alhallowes
Caſtle ſtret
Weſt ſtret

*Speed's map of Hertford, inset into his map of the county in 1610. It is the only representation we have of the Royal Castle and of the four churches which existed in the town. Note that Fore Street was then known as the "Highe Stret".*

## Introduction

The last century and a half has been a time of increasing rate of change in the way the people of Hertford live. Most of the population were once crowded in a small area in the centre; now the great majority live in the outer fringes of the town. The car has become a great convenience but equally a creator of problems. While the pattern of the town's streets centred on the Castle has remained unchanged, efforts continue to accommodate both people and motor traffic in them. The making of Gascoyne Way has taken heavy through traffic away from the town centre, though perhaps not far enough. Shopping habits are also much changed, especially since the Second World War. Gone are most of the small family shops, replaced by a few big stores. The rivers are no longer used for transport and as a source of power, as they were in the past, but they remain an amenity for townspeople and a home for wildlife, even in the centre of the town. It is the river valleys which give the town its "lungs" and Hertford remains a pleasant place in which to live. It is to be hoped that, in the endless process of evolution, it will remain so in the next century.

*A view of Fore Street in 1951 before there was any sign of one-way systems or traffic management. The photograph was later used by the police, who painted out the registration plates and listed all the traffic faults being committed. Note the large number of cyclists.*

# Fore Street and Parliament Square

Fore Street, shown on Speed's map as "Highe Stret", appears always to have been the town's main thoroughfare, wider than any of the other old streets. In it are the Post Office, the Corn Exchange, the Shire Hall, banks and offices. There are also some excellent shops, but they are scattered between the other buildings mentioned, so Fore Street could not be described as a busy shopping street. Parliament Square did not exist until the clearing for the War Memorial, but the row of cottages on the west side was called Parliament Row, commemorating the removal of Parliament to the Castle just behind them, due to the outbreak of plague in London in 1563.

*(Opposite top) This photograph taken well over 100 years ago shows the shape of the street much as it is today. The state of the road shows the need for crossings one of which may be seen in the distance. The iron frameworks seen on the pavement on the left were for shop awnings.*

*(Above) Originally all animals brought to market were sold in this street. In 1851 a new market was opened behind the Ram Inn with accommodation for 2,500 sheep, 500 pigs and space for calves. However there was no space for "horned cattle"; it must have been many years before this was provided - this picture can be no earlier than 1890.*

*(Opposite top)    This Corn Exchange was put up in the early 1840's; previously trading in corn was done at the back of the Shire Hall.*

*(This page, above)    The new Corn Exchange (illustrated over the page) was opened in 1859. Market Street and the covered market behind the Corn Exchange came about 1890. The shops shown here — Beard's men's outfitter and Savage the cooper and basket maker — had to be demolished.*

*(Opposite bottom)    These cottages in Railway Street were cleared for the other end of Market Street and the covered market.*

(Above)   The Shire Hall, designed in 1769 by James Adam (younger brother of Robert), was built as a Court House and has recently been restored as a modern magistrates' court.   But in its time it has been the centre of many town events—here the declaration of a parliamentary election result in 1898 when Evelyn Cecil was elected M.P.

(Opposite, top)   This picture shows the Corn Exchange as it was until the Second World War (apart from the lamps on the pavement which had long been removed).   Early in that war the figure of Ceres, the goddess of harvest, and the two decorative urns were removed as potential dangers to people below in the event of air raids.   Willson's next door was a wine shop.

(Bottom)   The Thistledoo Café on the Fore Street/Market Street corner was removed in the mid-1930's so that the Fore Street end of Market Street could be widened to make a bus stop.

*(Above) This building next to the Westminster (now National Westminster) Bank was the Post Office until the new one was built in 1890.*

*(Opposite, top) The Chequer Inn stood on this site which was bequeathed, with the yard behind, to Hertford's Poor Estate, a local charity. It was decided by the charity to build a post office on the site and lease it to the Government as a way of gaining income on their property.*

(Right) The Post Office was erected in 1890 by builder H. Norris for £2,000 and let to the Government for £120 per annum. After 21 years it was sold to the Government.

The original entry to the small public office was from Fore Street, the sorting office was behind and the telephone exchange on the first floor. After the building of a separate sorting office and exchange, it was changed to its present form with a side entrance to a larger public office.

Money was raised by public subscription to pay for the little tower on the top of the Post Office building. It must be assumed that this became the property of Hertford Poor Estate, and was sold to the Government with the rest of the building.

*A view from Castle Street before the War Memorial was built. The third building in from the right is the Blackbirds Inn. The Hertfordshire Mercury offices in Fore Street are partly visible.*

*This was a major clearance in the centre of the town to provide a site for the War Memorial. It was made possible by the generosity of Sir Edward Pearson of Brickenden Bury (see page 72), who presented the land for the memorial site to the town. The demolition had to be timed to match the provision of fresh accommodation for the dispossessed shopkeepers and other residents.*

*(Above) This view from Fore Street shows the buildings demolished to provide the site for the War Memorial.*

*(Below) The War Memorial before the cottages in Parliament Row gave way to shops. Simpson's, the printers, on the right was on the site of Briant's Bell Foundry.*

PARLIAMENT ROW, HERTFORD, 1928.
THE PREMISES OF MESSRS. SIMSON OCCUPY THE SITE OF JOHN BRIANT'S BELL FOUNDRY.

*Apart from shop windows, most of the right-hand side of the Wash looks much the same today. The left-hand side is completely different; the Castle Gates and Castle Hall have replaced all the buildings shown here — the Castle Cinema and the miller's house.*

## The Wash, the Castle and Old Cross

The low ground of the Wash, close to the river, must have been subject to flooding before the water was satisfactorily restrained. For the last century, at least, it has been a busy shopping area. In the days when Hertford was in two parts, joined by the ford, Old Cross was the "town centre" on the north side of the river. It was not till the end of the nineteenth century that there was finally free passage between the two parts, with the abolition of tolls on the bridge. The building of the bridge in 1927 with plenty of room for traffic flow has sealed the unity of the two parts of the town.

*(Above)  The Castle Gates were presented by Osmond Henry McMullen to "his native town" and opened by the Marquess of Salisbury in July 1912.*

*(Below)  This view of the Wash from Parliament Square was taken before the rebuilding of the Green Dragon and neighbouring premises.  The distant shops in the Wash have changed little.*

HERTFORD CASTLE.

*(Above)   What was originally the castle gatehouse is now referred to as the Castle.  Since this picture was taken, further building was added to the left side in the 1930's.*

*(Below)   For a period up to the Second World War, tennis courts were available for public hire in the Castle grounds.*

*(Above) Gascoyne Way now crosses the Lea at this spot near the Castle where boats could be hired.*

*(Below) Castle Street looks much like this today, though recent road works have made it into a cul-de-sac. The castellated building on the right is part of the offices occupied by Longmore's, the long-established firm of solicitors.*

*(Above)  On Boxing Day 1893, Mill Bridge was freed of the toll;  the ceremony was performed by the High Sheriff, Earl Cowper K.G., of Panshanger, and attended by the Mayor and Corporation.*

*(Opposite, top)  The buildings on the right of this view of the Wash from Mill Bridge are the house and shop attached to the Town Mill.  The lawn by the side of Castle Hall has taken their place.*

*(Bottom)  This was Mill Bridge until the present bridge was built in around 1927.  Next to the bridge is the small toll house — originally tolls were charged for all vehicles and animals such as horses, cows and donkeys crossing.*

*(Above)  This is the building which was demolished to provide a site for the Borough Library. The house on the extreme right remains and is used by McMullen's.*

*(Below)  The Borough Library was opened in 1888 by A.J. Balfour, who had been M.P. for Hertford and was later Prime Minister. The upper floors were a School of Art. The Borough retained the library until the early 1960's when it became a branch of the County Library Service.*

HERTFORD, MEMORIAL TABLET & FOUNTAIN. 36485

*(Above)   When excavations were made for the building of the Library, remains of the Church of St. Mary the Less were found and made into a drinking fountain.  The tablet on the Library wall lists all townsmen who volunteered and served in the South African War (see page 143).*

*(Below)   This method of road surfacing at Old Cross would present problems to today's traffic.*

*Honey Lane still provides a convenient passage from Maidenhead Street to Market Place and Fore Street.*

## Maidenhead Street to South Street

What we now know as Maidenhead Street and Railway Street, running parallel to Fore Street, was all called Back Street, according to Speed's map of 1610. Early on, the western part was known as Cordwainers' Street due to the number of leather-dressers in the area; its present name derives from the seventeenth-century Maidenhead Inn, which was on the site now occupied by Woolworth's store. Maidenhead Street became a busy shopping street with many food shops. The eastern end continued to be known as Back Street until the coming of the railway to the East station. With the adjacent Butcherley Green, this was a densely populated area, containing numerous insanitary houses. The coming of the supermarkets has diminished Maidenhead's shopping role, while Butcherley (now Bircherley) Green has become a shopping precinct and Railway Street has lost its slums. Market Place was the site of a market before the Shire Hall was built.

Hertford.  Maidenhead Street

*(Above)  Looking towards Bull Plain:  two well-known inns of the past can be seen in this view of Maidenhead Street in 1904 — the Green Dragon on the right and the Maidenhead, the signboard of which is further up on the left.*

*(Below)  Looking towards the Wash:  until the coming of supermarkets, Maidenhead Street was the chief shopping street in the town.  Honey Lane is behind the near cart on the left.*

MAIDENHEAD STREET, HERTFORD.

*(Above)   Honey Lane, like the rest of the town, was well provided with inns.  Here are two neighbouring houses — the Highland Chief and the Old Coffee House.  Visible in Maidenhead Street is Hilton's boot and shoe shop.*

*(Opposite, top)   A view of Bull Plain.  It took its name from the Bull Inn which may be seen on the left, approximately where Hertford Cameras is now.  In the distance is Lombard House, now occupied by the Hertford Club.*

*(Below)   This arcade of shops provided shopping under cover and gave pedestrians access from Bull Plain to Green Street and the old bus station and car park.  The arcade was in existence for about 50 years, between the two transformations of Bircherley Green.  The site is now taken by a goods entrance to the shops in Bircherley Green.*

*(Above)   This building occupied the open space in Salisbury Square - Graveson's can be seen on the left and the White Hart on the right.  In it were the Vine Inn, an education office and Quelch and Brown's cycle shop.  It was demolished in the 1920's.*

*(Below)   A corner of Salisbury Square.  The grocer's shop was finally Greaves' and is now a jeweller's.*

*(Above)   The Covered Market was built in about 1890 and closed in 1979.  On its demolition Railway Street was widened on this corner and business premises now occupy the rest of the site.*

*(Below)  Traffic lights controlled this crossing in Railway Street when this picture was taken; buses and cars crossed from Market Street on the right into Green Street on the left to go to the bus station and car park on Bircherley Green.  The Covered Market is on the right corner.*

*(Above)  This view of Railway Street dates from early this century; the building on the extreme right was a blacksmith's. The inn with the board outside was the Lion's Head. The exit from Butcherley Green was where the two girls are standing.*

*(Below)  This is Railway Street just before the building of the Bircherley Green shopping precinct. The street on the right was the exit from the bus station and car park, the opening by the white poster was the site of the open market on Saturdays.*

*(Above)   This is where the Earl Haig pub now stands at the corner of Railway Street and South Street. The date on the posters is 1914 and one of the street crossings so necessary on the dirty roads can be seen in front of the two boys.*

*(Below)   This photograph of the corner of South Street and Fore Street shows how much poor housing there was quite close to the centre of the town before the First World War.*

*At the entry to Hartham Lane was a sign pointing to Cowbridge Station. The big building in the background was Cowbridge House, now demolished except for the small part on the extreme right which remains as Hartham Chapel. The fenced garden also remains.*

# Northwards: Cowbridge to Bengeo

Cowbridge, leading off Old Cross, was the drovers' route for taking cattle in and out of the town. At the beginning of the last century, it has some mean housing called "Little Russia", in the part where Dimsdale Street is now. It crosses the Beane to an area at the bottom of Port Hill, which in the past suffered flooding on a number of occasions. While the main road turns right up the hill towards Bengeo, Port Vale goes straight on to the Molewood Road, the only way by which corn, flour, etc., could be taken in and out of Molewood Mill (Beane Road was not opened until 1922). There was also an entrance to Sele Mill off Port Vale. In the middle of the last century letters to the local paper spoke of the bad state of the road and footpath in Port Vale, one correspondent writing of a "slimy plethora which makes it difficult to decide if it is a road or a bog". Bengeo developed as a village separate from the town and still retains some of its distinctive character. It is an area of the town which has expanded greatly since the Second World War, and it is far enough out of the town for small shops still to function there.

*(Above)   A general view of Cowbridge early in this century, with characteristic gentle means of travel.   The church on the left, then Congregational, is now the United Reformed Church.*

*(Below)   Prince Albert Cottages were erected in Cowbridge in 1864 by the Hertford Building Company, an organisation concerned with better housing for the poor.   The design, by Henry Roberts, was first used on a site near the Great Exhibition of 1851, when Prince Albert provided the site and the money for the building.   The Hertford copy was built on land given by Baron Dimsdale. Each of the four cottages shown had a living room a scullery and three bedrooms, each of which had a separate entry, i.e. no bedroom was reached by passing through another.*

*(Above)  An easily recognisable view of Port Vale.  The Two Brewers pub was then supplied by the West Street brewery of Nicholls.*

*(Below)  This view of Port Vale looking towards the town shows Christ Church on the left, on the corner of Balfour Street.  The church has been replaced by houses, but the infants school building behind it remains as the Little Theatre of the Company of Players.*

*Some of Port Vale's past residents with a baker's roundsman and his delivery cart. The Old Mill Stream inn is visible in the background.*

Port Vale is a narrow road and became dangerous when increasing through traffic used it as a diversionary route. Some years ago, the problem was solved by blocking the road at the bottom end of Byde Street. In addition, parking space was provided for local inhabitants by the demolition of two houses. A number of cottages in the street have been modernised.

*(Above)    The Reindeer still refreshes the traveller before he ascends Port Hill.  The walled enclosure by its side is the Quaker Burial Ground, which is still there though no longer used.*

*(Below)  An attractive view of Port Hill from the top.*

*(Above)*     *A view of Fanshawe Street from Farquhar Street and across Byde Street. The house on the extreme right is the Old Pest House, which was built in 1763 "for the reception of persons, in Hertford and Bengeo, affected with smallpox in the natural way."*

*(Below) The railings in front of the old Bengeo schools are on the left of this view looking towards Port Hill. After the building of new schools elsewhere, flats have been built on the site.*

*(Above)   A scene in Bengeo Street when Bengeo was a country village.*

*(Below)   Duncombe Road before its completion with several children very willing to be in the picture.*

*The Ebenezer Strict Baptist Chapel stood at the junction of Hertingfordbury Road and North Road. This area has been altered out of all recognition by new roads, since this picture was taken in 1964.*

# Westwards: St. Andrew Street to Hertingfordbury

While St. Andrew Street remains relatively unaltered, Hertingfordbury Road as part of the A414 — an outer east/west route around the north of London — has changed completely. It is the link between Gascoyne Way and the Hertingfordbury by-pass; the latter has restored some peace to the village. Cross Lane, linking the A414 with North Road, has been widened to cope with the greatly increased flow of traffic.

St. Nicholas Hall was opened in 1893 as a parish hall; it is now occupied by Beckwith's antique shop. Money to build St. Nicholas Hall was raised in many ways. Some was raised by a fete in Christ's Hospital grounds, at which this balloon ascent was a great attraction. Other money came from people in Hartford, Connecticut. The name St. Nicholas came from a church in Maidenhead Street which fell into disuse, the parish of which was combined with that of St. Andrew.

St. Andrew Street, Hertford

Published by T. Levey, Hertford

*(Above) St. Andrew Street from a point on the town side of St. Nicholas Hall. The house with steps is now, like many other premises in the street, a shop selling antiques.*

*(Below) The building of St. Nicholas Hall. The old cottage, dating from the 15th century, next to the footpath, remains, with its timbers now uncovered. The other cottages, which stood on the site of the tithe barn, were taken down and St. Nicholas Hall built on the site.*

*(Above)   A view into St. Andrew Street from Hertingfordbury Road taken in 1964. The large house "Cawthorne" and the two cottages opposite it are the only surviving buildings after the road changes.*

*(Below)   This was Hertingfordbury Road before the dual carriageway was made.  The Sele Road corner is visible to the right of the lorry*

*(Above)  This shows the extent of the widening of Cross Lane in the road changes made to cater for modern traffic needs.  St. Andrew's Rectory on the extreme left lost some of its garden.*

*(Below)  This view in North Road in 1904 shows the elegance of this crescent of houses. The ground on the left was a nursery.*

THE COUNTY HOSPITAL, HERTFORD.

*(Above) The County Hospital was opened as the General Infirmary in 1833. Many extensions have been added since this picture was taken. Now the hospital faces closure, a process which has already started.*

*(Below) North Road showing the entrances to the hospital and Sele Mill. The Ekins board in Sele Road suggests a date of 1919 when the Camps Hill council estate was being built.*

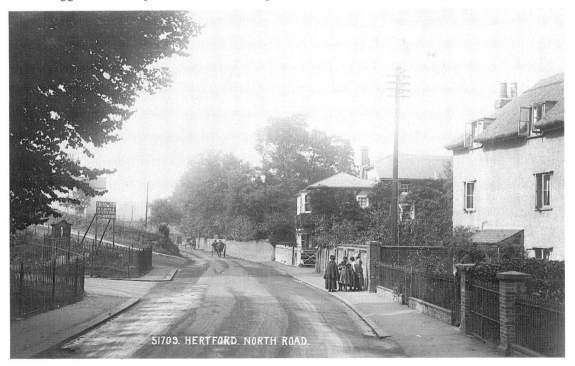

51709. HERTFORD. NORTH ROAD.

*(Above) This bridge over North Road carried the line from Cowbridge Station to Welwyn. The direction post at the bottom of Welwyn Road can be seen in the distance.*

*(Below) West Street has retained much of its character over the years and now has extra peace due to the absence of through traffice since the the building of Gascoyne Way.*

Published by Rose & Sons, Hertford    S³206    *Hertingfordbury Village*

(Above) Hertingfordbury village before cars were common, with the White Horse ready to provide refreshment for man and horse.

(Below) Cowper Memorial Hall, Hertingfordbury, was provided as a village hall. It passed out of village possession some years ago and is now known as Mayflower Place.

THE COWPER MEMORIAL HALL, HERTFORD    37441

*Rooks Alley ran from the top of the Mangrove Road hill to Fore Street. This part, where it crosses Hagsdell Road, remains but the lower part has been driven underground by Gascoyne Way.*

# Southwards: the London Road to Church Street

To the south is high land above one side of the valley in which the town centre lies. All Saints' Church, the "parish church", is now separated from the centre by Gascoyne Way. At a time when education was closely linked with the Church, there were six schools in a line to the east of All Saints'. Now only one remains, the others having been replaced by buildings on the top of the high ground. County Hall was built on the same ridge of high ground.

*(Opposite, top) The London Road is on the left with Mangrove Road on the right. When the Cowper School was built in 1841, the newspaper account reported that it was "by the house of Mr. Hale the gardener". A later Mr. Hale made cycles to order; he was also a coach builder.*

*(Bottom) In this later photograph, the Cowper School can be seen but Mr. Hale's house at the road junction has gone. On the extreme right the wooden archway marks Mr. Hale's new place of business. He continued making cycles and carriage building here, then turned to the care of cars. The Hale family continues a motor business here and in Ware.*

*(Above)   This is the start of the building of the Queen's Road houses seen from higher up the hill.*

*(Below)   Queen's Road completed.  A view up Queen's Road early in this century.*

*(Opposite page, top)   A view southwards along Church Street.  Samuel Neale lived in the Old Vicarage at the top of Church Street and opened his garage next door.  Later Neale's Garage moved to London Road, but a garage building remains in Church Street.*

*(Bottom)   A view of Church Street, looking northwards through the iron gates from All Saints' churchyard.  Fore Street and the side of the Shire Hall are in the background.*

Hertford Union, Ware Road, Hertford.

*This building in Ware Road was built as a workhouse; after its use for this purpose, it became a boarding school for boys with learning difficulties. The police station now occupies the site. The clock from the tower of the workhouse and school was put into All Saints' Church tower.*

# Eastwards: Ware Road

Ware is a mere three miles to the east, and the two towns have almost joined, especially to the south of Ware Road. To the north, the marshy ground of the Meads precludes any building.

Two roads off Ware Road, Fairfax and Cromwell by name, together with Cockbush Avenue, recall an incident which happened hereabouts in the Civil War. In 1647, with discontent fomenting among Roundhead troops, Cromwell and Fairfax rode out from Hertford to review their troops parading in the Cockbush Field. One of the regiments had papers in the hats proclaiming "England's freedom and soldiers' rights" and at first refused to remove them. But the mutiny was brought to an end when three ringleaders were seized and sentenced to death. In the end, the three were allowed to draw lots to decide which of them should die; finally, one of them, Arnold, was at the head of the regiment.

*(Opposite, top) The view eastwards along the tree-lined Ware Road. The old workhouse building is visible in the distance. The Methodist Church on the left is now in a new building.*

*(Bottom) The Plough Hotel at the corner of Ware Road and London Road (now Old London Road) early in this century. In the 1930's a new Plough Hotel was built further back and the road widened. The new building, after being renamed The Warehouse, has now been replaced by an office block. This area of the town was once known as "World's End".*

*(Above)   From the corner of Baker Street the buildings of Christ's Hospital can be seen.  The wooden fence in the foreground is in front of the site of the Chapel, not then built.*

*(Below)   The Chapel of Christ's Hospital Girls' School;  this site is now used as a car park by Tesco's.*

*The western section of Gascoyne Way. This shows the section from St. Andrew Street to Castle Street under construction. There was still direct access for traffic from Castle Street to West Street; but on completion of the bypass, Castle Street became a cul-de-sac.*

## Gascoyne Way: a Mixed Blessing

In the mid 1960's Gascoyne Way was constructed to provide a bypass for traffic wishing to avoid the centre of the town. Above and on the next page are two pictures, which show the extent of the project. As the bypass passed close to the town centre, demolitions and some loss of amenity were inevitable. This chapter therefore also shows what was lost — from a series of photographs taken in May-June 1964, before the work started, showing some of the areas affected. Gascoyne Way was always controversial — and still is. In the 1990's, it was found that at certain times of each day congestion on Gascoyne Way was so great that motorists were using the town centre to by-pass the by-pass — as a result new traffic management schemes were being tried out.

*(Above)   The eastern section of Gascoyne Way.  In the foreground is the Hale Road roundabout; Hale Road provides access to County Hall and Queen's Road.  There is also access to the town centre from the roundabout.*

*(Below)   This row of large houses opposite Christ's Hospital buildings has all gone.  Inland Revenue and other offices were located on the ground floors, the upper floors were used for accommodation, some for Christ's Hospital staff.  At the far end of the row was Elliott's music shop. The farthest building visible was Hertford Motors, now the site of the Iceland store.*

*(Opposite, top) The shops and houses on the right are part of the property demolished in St. Andrew Street. In front of the spire can be seen the top of the house "Cawthorne", which was preserved.*

*(Bottom) This view from the opposite direction shows "Cawthorne" on the left. The rest of the property visible on that side of the road has gone, including the Red Lion Inn.*

*(Above)* *This end of Water Lane together with the building on the left, the Black Swan Inn, is now under Gascoyne Way.*

*(Opposite, top)* *Castle Street/West Street Junction from Castle Street. Castle Street passed into West Street by a small S bend, the start of which is seen here.*

*(Bottom)* *From West Street: on the right is the forecourt of what was originally known as Chaseside Garage (after several other names it is now called Trimoco). The Gladstone Arms was demolished and the end of Pegs Lane was "sealed off".*

*(Above)   The main entrace to Hertford Grammar School (now Richard Hale) was by a long road from Castle Street.  The route of this road is now crossed by Gascoyne Way and Hale Road, with Sovereign House between.*

*(Below)   From All Saints' tower, Church Street can be seen with a gate at its end leading into the churchyard.  Gascoyne Way now passes between the church and the cottage in the foreground, taking over much of the churchyard to the north of the church.*

*(Above)  The Longmore School is in the foreground, the building with the small turret being the original Hale's Grammar School. Gascoyne Way carves through the land to the north of the school to the point opposite the Christ's Hospital buildings, which can be seen at the top of the picture. This picture and the previous one show how many trees were felled when the road was made.*

*(Below)  This shows the junction of Ware Road and London Road (now called Old London Road). To the left is Neale's Garage, to the right the Plough Inn.  The car park in the foreground was once part of the Plough Field.*

*Butcherley (now Bircherley) Green was one of the most crowded areas in Hertford. Part of it can be seen in this picture from Folly Island, looking across the Lee Navigation Canal. In the distance is the tower of All Saints' Church.*

## Courts, Alleys and Yards

In 1849 the town suffered an outbreak of cholera which caused a number of deaths. The Borough Sanitary Committee produced a report on some housing which gave these facts:

| | | |
|---|---|---|
| Number of Courts, Alleys and Yards | 42 | |
| Number of cottages in these yards | 294 | (of which only 28 had back doors.) |
| Population of the yards | 1310 | |
| Number of closets | 102 | (mostly over cesspools) |
| Number of pumps and wells for cottages | 19 | |

Much of the rest of the town's housing was poor. There was immediate work to improve sanitation but the problem of over-crowding was not really tackled until after World War I, when council houses were build out of the middle of the town.

*(Opposite, top)  Another view across the canal. These cottages on the "Green" remained well into the 1920's.  On the extreme left is the Ragged School with the Tallow House to the right of it.*

*(Bottom)   The Tallow House, where candles were made, in the corner of the "Green".  The chimneys seen between the building are of houses on Folly Island.*

*(Above)   These houses off Green Street were demolished in 1905.*

*(Opposite page, top)   Hayden's Court was in Railway Street in the region of the Friends' Meeting House.  It lasted into the 1920's.*

*(Bottom)   A view of Maidenhead Yard which was behind the Maidenhead Inn in Maidenhead Street. It is now a car park at the back of Woolworth's.*

Although the housing in these courts, alleys and yards was very poor, there was often a strong community spirit among the families living in them, and a tradition of mutual help in adversity.

*(Above)   This was Dolphin Yard off Maidenhead Street.*

*(Opposite page, top)   Chequer Yard, sometimes known as Paradise Court, was badly affected by the cholera outbreak.  It went with the building of the Post Office on the site in 1892.*

*(Bottom)   This yard off St. Andrew Street is euphemistically called Poet's Corner on the slide from which this print was taken.  The trees in the background were in the Castle grounds.*

*The Satin Drawing Room of Balls Park when it was the private residence of the Faudel Phillips family — photograph copyright the Royal Commission of Historical Monuments for England.*

# Big Houses

Hertford is surrounded by "big houses" and until the Second World War most of them were lived in by families who had the wealth to keep them in good condition and staff them with servants. Since the war, most of these houses have become offices or institutions of one sort or another. Balls Park is the nearest surviving "big house" to the centre of Hertford. In the earlier part of the last century it was occupied by Marquess Townshend and his family, then until the Second World War by the Faudel-Phillips family, who figured prominently in the life of the town. After the war, it became a College of Education for training schoolmistresses, and now it is part of the University of Hertfordshire. Part of the extensive grounds about the house are occupied by Simon Balle Comprehensive School and its playing fields.

*(Above)   The exterior of Balls Park*

*(Below)   For many years Goldings belonged to the Abel Smith family who gave to Waterford its lovely little church with its unique collection of stained glass from the William Morris school. In more recent times it was used by Dr. Barnardo's, teaching young men printing, gardening and tin-smithing; now it is used by Hertfordshire County Council.*

"PANSHANGER", HERTFORD.

*(Above)   The exterior of Panshanger, when it was the home of Lord Desborough.*

*(Below)   The Large Orangery at Panshanger, photographed in 1951 — photograph copyright the Royal Commission of Historical Monuments for England.*

*The staircase at Panshanger, photographed in 1953; the door led to the Picture Gallery — photograph copyright the Royal Commission of Historical Monuments for England.*

Panshanger was the grandest of the big houses near Hertford. It lay on the other side of the Mimram valley from Hertingfordbury and was the home of the Earls Cowper. As well as the house, built in the Gothick style in 1806, there was an extensive estate, laid out by Humphrey Repton. The First World War left the Cowper family without heirs and the house passed to Lord Desborough. On his death, the estate was split up and the house totally demolished in 1953-54.

Morgan's Walk Near Hertford                                      30366

(*Above*)   *Epcombs is one of the few big houses which remain private residences, and is in the possession of the Thompson-McCausland family.   This attractive house at Hertingfordbury is supposed to have been Jane Austen's model for "Longbourn", the home of the Bennets in her novel "Pride and Prejudice".*

(*Opposite, top*)   *The drive leading to Brickendon Bury.  Sir Alfred Pearson, who was Mayor of Hertford in 1922, was the last resident of the house which is now occupied by Malaysian Rubber Producers Research Association.*

(*Bottom*)   *Leahoe was built as a private residence and continued as such into this century; it later became a convent.  It was purchased, with its grounds, by Hertfordshire County Council in 1934 and County Hall was built on the purchased ground.  The house has been retained and is used for offices and as a social club for County Hall staff.*

*The sailing barge seen here is on the Lee Navigation canal, which was cut in the 18th century to enable malt to be carried by river from Hertford to the London brewers and other goods brought back. It was made by enlarging the millstream for the Priory Mill (later called the Dicker Mill), and thus created an island, Folly Island, between it and the River Lea. The nearer malting and the buildings in front of it belonged to the Lombard House, the corner of which can be seen on the extreme right.*

## Rivers and Mills

Hertford's four rivers, the Lea and its tributaries the Mimram, the Beane and the Rib, had a great influence on the kind of town Hertford became. In the distant past, they carved out valleys in which the town lies. The ford across the Lea gave the site strategic importance. Over many years the rivers provided a means of conveying goods for trade, and gave power to the six mills which worked in the town. Before their closing, all mills had other power sources to replace or supplement water power.

*(Opposite, top) The Lombard House can be seen more fully in this photograph. Through the bridge is the point where the canal leaves the Lea. Barges carrying timber, etc. passed under the bridge, then to the right where there were wharves for unloading.*

*(Bottom) The Priory Wharf situated at the "widewater" was much more convenient for the delivery of building materials, and the Andrew brothers, builders, ceased using the Folly Island site in favour of this. When the Andrew brothers retired in 1896 the wharf and the works were sold to Ewen and Tomlinson, and were finally held by Jewson's. It is many years since goods were delivered here and this piece of water is now a marina for the mooring of privately-owned boats.*

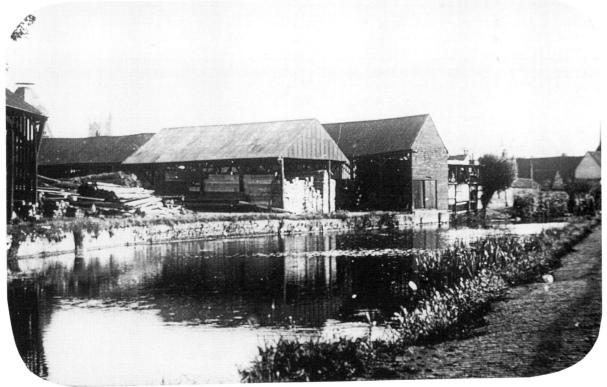

*(Opposite page, above)  Hertford Lock: this is an essential part of the navigation canal ensuring the necessary depth of water while adjusting for the fall in the river between the points where the canal leaves and rejoins.  The large building in the distance is Ware Park Mill.*

*(Bottom)  The Ware Park Mill was built in 1721 by James Fordham. It used the waters of the Rib which fell steeply here, and was the only over-shot mill in Hertford. It was used for grinding corn and by the nineteenth century belonged to the Ware miller, J.W. French and Co. It will be seen that there were also maltings on the site.*

*(Above on this page)  A view of Ware Park Mill from just above the point where the navigation and the old river join.*

NEAR DICKER'S MILL, HERTFORD

Dicker Mill.    ElectricWorks.    GramophoneFactory. Bowden Hertford.

*(Above)   Molewood Mill was included in the Domesday Book entry for Bengeo.  It continued as a corn mill until 1888 when it was bought by Hertford Corporation to establish a pumping station for the town's water supply.  The miller's house remains.*

*(Opposite, top)   Dicker Mill, originally Priory Mill, had moved downstream from its position by the Priory in about 1630.  In its later years, it was entirely an oil mill, extracting oil from such seeds as linseed and pressing the remaining material into cake for feeding cattle.  It closed in the 1920's.*

*(Bottom)   Another view of Dicker Mill with other industrial premises — the electric works and gramophone factory — which sprang up nearby.*

(Above)  Sele Mill is recorded in the Domesday Book.  At the end of the fifteenth century the first paper mill in England was established here by John Tate, but this lasted only a few years.  It was a corn mill for most of its time and in 1889 new machinery was installed replacing stones by rollers. In 1890 a fire which burned for three days destroyed the mill.  The picture shows that the miller's house escaped serious damage.

(Opposite, top)  After the fire, Sele Mill was rebuilt away from the house. The Garratt family owned the mill from 1866 and continued to grind corn there until 1988 when they moved the business to Lincolnshire. Milling continued for a short time but the mill has been unused for several years. The miller's house was made into flats years before the mill closed.

(Bottom)  Flooding of the River Lea at the Port Vale, Nelson Street, Molewood Road and Beane Road crossroads.

(Above)  Hornsmill is recorded in Domesday Book. In the early nineteenth century it ground corn, crushed oil seed and ground bones for fertiliser. By the mid 1800's it converted to producing oil and cake only and in 1858 was rebuilt and equipped with the latest machinery.  By 1890 oil production ceased and the premises were sold to leather-dresser William Webb.

(Below)   At first only chamois leather was produced, but later a thriving glove making business developed;  this is a picture of a workshop in the factory.  The business closed in 1971 and streets of houses now cover the site of the mill and its surrounding property.

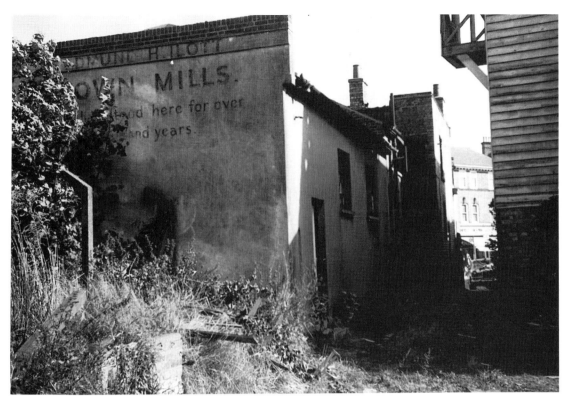

(*Above and below*) *The Town Mill was also recorded in the Domesday Book. It seems to have been solely a corn mill throughout, converting to rollers in the last century. It was bought by Edmund Ilott of Harpenden in 1855; he put the mill in charge of his 14 year-old son who became a master miller by the age of 21. The mill remained in the Ilott family until the death of Percy. On the side wall was a sign saying "a mill stood here for over a thousand years." It was demolished to make way for Castle Hall.*

*(Above)   The platforms of Hertford East Station when steam trains were still running.  The line is now electrified, using overhead cables.*

# Railways

The branch railway to Hertford from Broxbourne, on the London to Cambridge line, was opened in October 1843.  In order to keep the railway at some distance from both Hertford Gaol and Christ's Hospital School, the original station was built several hundred yards nearer Ware than the present one.   The new station was opened in 1888 and renamed Hertford East after the opening of the Hertford North line to King's Cross.

*(Opposite, top)  The ornate facade of Hertford East Station, opened in 1888 with a porch for horse-drawn carriages to drive into.*

*(Below)  Cowbridge Station came into use in 1858 with the completion of a branch line off the Great Northern Railway at Welwyn.  A few years later, the junction was moved to Hatfield.*

Hertford Station G. E. R

*(Above)* Another view of Cowbridge Station from Hartham Lane, with McMullen's Brewery on the right. When the station closed on the opening of Hertford North, the building was used by McMullen's and has only recently been taken down.

*(Below)* The platform at Cowbridge Station. The line provided Hertford with access to trains to the North of England, as well as giving another service to London.

*(Above) Another view of the platform at Cowbridge, with McMullen's Brewery in the background.*

*(Below) The start of Hertford North Station. The loop off the Great Northern line from Alexandra Palace to Stevenage was started before the First World War and completed in about 1920. This shows the first stages in the building of Hertford North Station, opened in 1924. The making of Beane Road and the development of housing estates at the west end of the town came with the station.*

*McMullen's Brewery wagons, decorated for the traditional Whit-Monday parade on Hartham Common, photographed at the turn of the century.*

# Malting, Brewing and Inns

Malting has long been a major industry in East Hertfordshire. To produce malt, barley grains are soaked and spread on a floor, where germination changes the starch in the grains into sugar. Germination is stopped when the grain is roasted in kilns — the cowls on the top of the kilns were once a major feature of the Hertford landscape. In the brewing process, the sugar in the malt is extracted into solution, then fermented by adding the plant, yeast, which feeds on the sugar, yielding alcohol in its place. In the past, there were a number of breweries in the town and many of the inns brewed their own beer; some of the large private houses also had their own brewhouses. Now one brewery remains, an all too rare example of an independent family business, and the number of inns has greatly decreased.

*(Opposite, top and bottom) Two views of Young's brewery, which was opened in 1754. It was sold in 1896 and ceased brewing in 1897, when it was taken down and its site absorbed into Christ's Hospital grounds. The wall with cellar openings remains in South Street today.*

*(Above) The Hope Brewery in Hartham Lane, which was taken over and incorporated in the bigger McMullen's Brewery in 1890.*

*(Opposite, top) Wickham's brewery was at Mill Bridge on the opposite side of the river from where Castle Hall now stands. It ceased brewing in the mid 1930's and its few "houses" were taken over by Wells & Winch.*

*(Bottom) Nicholl's brewery was in West Street; the archway by the brewer's house led to the brewery which was demolished in 1965. The site is now occupied by houses.*

*(Above)   Eric Taylor was the last cooper employed by McMullen's; he is seen at work in 1955 with some of his handiwork.  He died in 1988.*

*(Opposite, top)  McMullen's brewery opened in 1830 on the site at Millbridge, now occupied by the Woolpack.  This was the company's original bill head, which emphasized their role as coopers and dealers in malt and hops almost as prominently as brewers of ale and beer.  Originally ale was not flavoured by hops, while beer was.*

*(Bottom)   The new bill head shows the new premises in Hartham Lane into which McMullen's moved in about 1890.  These premises incorporated the former Hope Brewery (illustrated on a previous page).  It will be seen that McMullen's had their own maltings to supply the brewery.*

(Above) *Originally all deliveries from the brewery were made by horse-drawn drays. This picture taken in 1948 shows the last pair of dray horses - the driver was Bill Ball.*

(Opposite, top) *This picture of a "Yorkshire" steam wagon was taken in 1924. Though another of McMullen's steam wagons is occasionally seen about the town on special occasions, all deliveries are now made by lorry.*

(Bottom) *A McMullen's delivery lorry of the 1960's, with bodywork for the Austin chassis made by Denver Motor Bodies of Barwick Ford, near Ware.*

*The Bell Inne at Hertford*                    Rowlandson 1

(Above)   The Cold Bath was originally further out of Hertford, opposite the end of Cross Lane, where it had a theatre and field where circuses could perform.   The building shown was at the junction of North Road and Hertingfordbury Road, opposite the Ebenezer Chapel.   Now the new Ebenezer Chapel is on the site of the demolished inn.

(Opposite page, top)    The Bell was purchased by the Marquess of Salisbury and became the Salisbury Arms. It was the Tory headquarters in the 1832 election, when the bribery and corruption were so great that the election was declared void and Hertford was unrepresented for several years. The picture is by Thomas Rowlandson and shows also the King's Head Hotel, where Millett's shop is now.

(Opposite, bottom)    The Dimsdale Arms was originally the Duncombe Arms and was the headquarters of Tom Duncombe and his fellow Whig candidate in the notorious election of 1832.

*(Above)   For a period, the Woolpack was called the Newbridge Inn.   This view of one of the bars shows some of the 7000 cigarette cards which were displayed by a pre-war landlord, Harry D. Wimblett.*

*(Opposite, top)   The Traveller's Rest was on the corner of Cowbridge and Dimsdale Street.  The building has since served a number of purposes and is now "Bob Hill Motor Cycles".  The main structure is unchanged and is well maintained.*

*(Bottom)   The Cross Keys in Fore Street had extensive cellars, over some of which the Corn Exchange was built.  These continued to be used by the wine shops which occupied the Cross Keys' site until the putting of shops into the Corn Exchange site.*

*The celebratory dinner for the Directors, employees and suppliers of Stephen Austin & Sons, held in the Shire Hall on the day in 1954 when new premises were opened in Caxton Hill.*

# The Place of Work

As a market town, Hertford has developed industries concerned with the produce of the land in milling, malting, brewing and leather dressing, rather than any form of heavy industry. Printing and later the making of gloves and brushes occupied a moderate number of people. Others have been employed in providing services to their fellows in the town but many have had to travel to other places of work. Since the coming of the railway, London has provided work for many people while, in later years, the more industrialised towns of Welwyn Garden City, Hatfield and Stevenage have provided work for others. Four local firms of different character are considered here.

Printing has long been a Hertford industry and for over 200 years Stephen Austin has been pre-eminent in that industry. Stephen Austin came to Hertford in 1768 and the Austin family carried on the business until 1909, when Victor Harrison took over. It was Stephen Austin's business connection with the East India College at Haileybury which led to the firm's facility to print foreign languages, in which it established a world-wide reputation. From 1772, Stephen Austin produced a local newspaper, a production which it continued until a few years ago when it sold its interest in the *Hertfordshire Mercury*. The firm's operations are now conducted from modern offices in Caxton Hill, off the Ware Road, which were opened on 10th November, 1954.

(Above)    The firm started in Hertford in premises in Maidenhead Street, moving in 1836 to Fore Street. In 1854 it moved to these premises, also in Fore Street, where the Hertfordshire Mercury is still edited.

(Right) At the opening of the new Caxton Hill premises, traditional practice was followed and junior apprentices poured beer on the four corners of the building under the supervision of the Father of the Chapel (Mr. R.L. Marshall) who then drank to the success of their works. The apprentice on the right is Ken Hartfield, the present Managing Director of Stephen Austin.

*Addis came to Hertford after the First World War, moving into this site in the Ware Road in 1919
and taking over the buildings of the Hertford Steam Laundry, seen in the centre of this page. The
tanks in the field behind this building were for storing under water the inflammable celluloid then*

*used in the manufacture of brush handles. In the top right corner of the photograph part of the old Militia Barracks may be seen — the Fire Service Headquarters now occupy the site. The bottom right shows some of the streets of houses which were built on the site of Hertford Gaol.*

*(Above)* *The Addis frontage in the Ware Road. The building on the right was put up in the 1930's and the rest after the Second World War. The firm which had concentrated on tooth brushes since the eighteenth century, now makes brushes of all sorts as well as other household products. In 1993, the firm decided to close the factory and transfer all work to its other factories, principally in Wales.*

*(Opposite page, top)* *For better quality tooth brushes, natural material such as bone was used. Here handles are being shaped.*

*(Bottom)* *In preparation of animal bristles for brushes it was essential to remove all traces of parasites. The ladies here are engaged in nit picking of a very practical sort.*

*(Above)  Ekins & Co. Ltd, Builders, was founded in 1803 and continues to offer its services today at its Great Northern Works. In earlier days all joinery needed was done in this workshop. Leaning against the distant wall is part of a screen made for St. Edmund's College*

In the last quarter of the nineteenth century, a number of public buildings were put up in the town and there was some house building too. House-building accelerated after the First World War with the erection of council estates and again since 1950, with more council houses and later a large number of private houses. Building firms of sufficient size were required to meet this increased demand — among them Andrews, Ekins, Norris, Castle, Ginn and Collins. Some of these firms finished long ago, some more recently, and a few remain. Of this last group the firm of Ekins & Co is featured here.

*(Opposite page, top)  The house at Ware Park was badly damaged by fire in July 1911 and Ekins were responsible for the repairs. The house was later used as a sanatorium for tuberculosis sufferers.*

*(Bottom)  In 1919 these men were engaged in building the council estate on Camps Hill, i.e. Sele Road etc. In 1968, the firm of Ekins was again on the estate, modernising the houses it had erected earlier.*

(Above)   For many years, the Dye family met a widespread need in sweeping the chimneys of the town and district. Central heating and the use of fuels other than coal and wood have greatly reduced that need. This is Daniel Dye senior, prepared to travel to houses in the district.

(Right)   This is David Dye, brother of Daniel senior, outside the firm's premises in Green Street, with the tools of his trade.

*(Above)  Boys were initiated into the trade by their heads being put into a bag of soot, but they were no longer sent up chimneys.  Tragedy struck the Dye family in 1844 when seven year old James Dye suffocated in a flue at Goldings.*

*(Below)  Daniel Dye junior is at the wheel of more modern transport with his father at his side. The younger Daniel was Mayor of Hertford and established a thriving coach business running concurrently with the chimney sweeping.  He died in 1964 and the business closed soon afterwards.*

*(Above)   Neale's furnishing store and Munnings' china shop occupied one of the best known buildings in Hertford. The magnificent pargetted building has recently been refurbished and is now a building society office.*

# Shops and Shopkeepers

The motor car and the supermarket have together had a radical effect on the shops of Hertford. Where there were many small shops selling food, now there are very few. The development of large out-of-town stores has affected shops of all types. What shops will flourish in the town in twenty years time?

*(Opposite, top)   One of the shops known as "Grocer & Provision Merchant" once so numerous, now disappeared. This one was at Mill Bridge.*

*(Bottom)   This shop at the lower end of Byde Street added a post office service to its provision of food.*

*(Above)   The interior of Graveson's store, in its fashionable heyday.*

From the end of the eighteenth century, Hertford's major drapery and clothing store was in the hands of three Quaker families, named Pollard, Robinson and Graveson.  At the end of the nineteenth century, the house on the corner of Maidenhead Street was taken down and the shop extended, under the name of Graveson and Robinson.  In 1899 the brothers William and Alfred Graveson took complete control of the business.  A limited company was formed in 1924, with William as Governing Director.  In addition to his business interests, William was prominent in Borough and County affairs and was a very keen naturalist.

*(Opposite page, top)   The view of the house and old shop which later became Graveson's — seen from Salisbury Square, with Maidenhead Street on the right.*

*(Bottom)   Graveson and Robinson, showing the extension replacing the house.*

*(Above) It is a little difficult to find a word to describe this shop on the opposite corner to Spencer's. It appeared to sell everything, except food and clothes. The building now matches the Spencer Corner and is occupied by Ladbroke's.*

*(Below) This jeweller's shop at the Parliament Square end of Fore Street was originally "Field and Marks". It later moved to the next door shop on the right, while this became a café, now an Indian restaurant.*

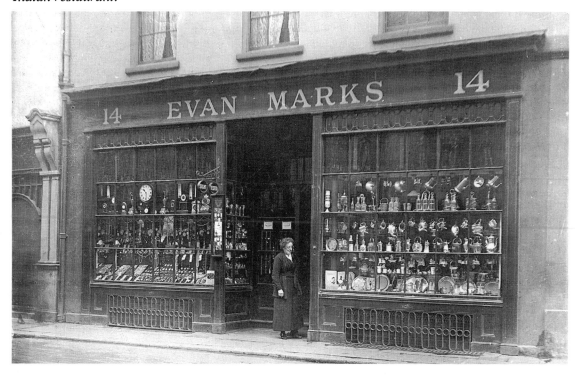

(Left) A gentlemen's outfitter at the corner of Maidenhead Street and the Wash. The building is little changed today although in recent years it has sold food—as a Wimpy Bar and, until 1993, as the Zeus Fish and Chip Bar.

(Right) Pateman's dairy and café in St. Andrew Street photographed in August 1925, with George Pateman and Gladys Bedwell in the milk-cart and Tom Pateman holding the horse. In the background to the left are Mr. and Mrs. F. Wackett outside their cycle shop.

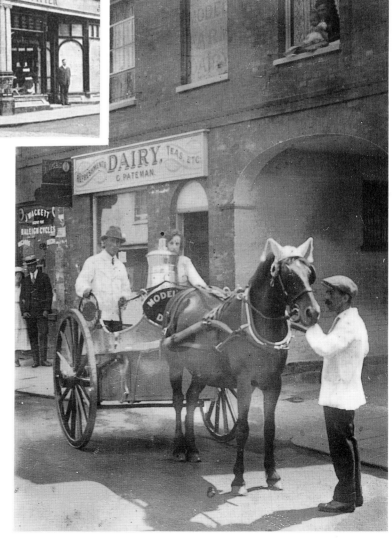

*(Above)  Two fine shops in Fore Street pictured early this century.  The Egyptian style building, now an Italian restaurant, was the shop of Gilbertson and Page, selling game food, dog biscuits, etc. It later became Bates Brothers, Grocers. Next door in the building which is now Midland Bank was Taylor's hardware shop.*

*(Opposite, top)  Gilbertson and Page's premises in Market Street:  later they had a factory in Tamworth Road.*

*(Bottom)  This shop may be called "the first of many". It is the original Beckwith's shop seen in 1907, when skilled craftsmen were employed on restoration work.  Since that day antique shops have taken over much of St. Andrew Street and Beckwith's has moved to St. Nicholas Hall; but other antique dealers use part of these premises at Old Cross. In the foreground is the ill-fated oak tree, planted in 1897 — its story is told on page 142.*

# The Johnsons' 104 years as butchers

*(Opposite, top) This picture of Hertford Market shows a butcher's stall on which the title "Redhead of Peterborough" may be deciphered. The staff manning this stall travelled to Cowbridge Station with their meat early on Saturday mornings, returning to Peterborough in the evening. In 1876, one of these men, Herbert Johnson, decided to leave Peterborough and set up business on his own in Hertford.*

*(Bottom) This is the shop established by Herbert Johnson in Railway Place; he is the central figure, his son Tom who was to carry on the business is on the right. The display shown was for Christmas 1908 and the meat which is marked "fed by his Majesty the King" came from Windsor.*

*In 1934, the business moved into this new shop at 21 Ware Road. The design of this shop prompted an article in the trade journal* Modern Meat Marketing, *in which the curved glass front was the main feature described. The author wondered whether this unique design, intended for the better display of meat on sale, would become popular. The proprietor Tom is on the right, with his eldest son Tom on the left and second son Bruce in the centre. The youngest son Jack was also in the business. The body of the van was made by Hale's Garage in London Road.*

*THE STORY CONTINUES ON THE NEXT PAGE ...*

# The Johnsons' 104 years as butchers

*For its final years, the business was conducted by Bruce helped by his wife, "Teddy". There were occasionally other assistants but none remained for long. Finally, in July 1980, Bruce and Teddy retired. The shop remained a butcher's for only a short while longer and now sells cane furniture.*

Arthur Elsden and his son, Arthur Vincent, ran a photographic business in Hertford from 1859 until 1926, and a number of their photographs are reproduced in this book. Arthur took over these premises in North Road, now part of Water's Garage, from a Mr. Craddock who had started in 1857. Arthur was a cabinet maker and made "mahogany and brass" type cameras; he would instruct purchasers in the practicalities of photography. In 1872, the two photographers moved to Mill Bridge, closing in 1926 when demolition of their later premises preceded the building of the new Mill Bridge. Note the sign saying "Elsden Photographist", rather than Photographer.

*(Above)  This is the interior of the Friends' Meeting House in Railway Street.  Built in 1669 it is reputed to be the oldest surviving purpose-built Friends' House in the world.*

# Churches

While the churches of St. Andrew and All Saints are comparatively new buildings, there were churches on their sites from early times.  Three other early churches existed — at the east end of the town St. John's which amalgamated with All Saints;  St. Mary the Less, remains of which were found when the Library was built and which were made into a drinking fountain (see page 25);  and St. Nicholas, which was a site at the back of the present Woolworth's store in Maidenhead Street and whose font is now in Tonwell Church.  The parishes of the latter two churches were absorbed into that of St. Andrew's.

Non-conformism has long been strong in the town.  John Wesley visited on a number of occasions, though he was not greatly impressed by the response he received.  There have been many Quakers prominent in the affairs of the town, their contribution to education including two schools — "three Quaker ladies" were responsible for founding the School of Industry for Girls (see pages 132-3) while William Pollard provided the funds for building the Ragged School (see page 134).  The Roman Catholic Church is in the area where the Priory was and it, too, has maintained a school.

Bengeo Parish Church near Hertford.

*(Above) St. Leonard's is the oldest church building in the town, dating from the early 12th century, probably built on the site of an earlier church. It is not in regular use, but services are held here occasionally*

*(Right) Holy Trinity Church, built in 1855, is now the Bengeo Parish Church.*

*(Above)   The old All Saints' Church, which was destroyed by fire in December 1891.  The fire appears to have been started by an overheated stove pipe.*

*(Opposite, top)   This photograph shows how complete was the destruction of All Saints' Church in the fire of 1891.*

*(Bottom)   The new All Saints', without the tower, was completed in 1895 — the Victoria Tower was completed in 1905.  The new building has developed faults over the years since it was built, and is now in need of repairs costing a few hundreds of thousands of pounds.  Efforts to raise the money to pay for the work have met with some success, but there is still much money to be found.*

(Above)   This is St. Andrew's Church before 1861.  At that time, the church was in such a poor condition that a decision was made to pull it down and build a new one. The demolition was carried out by the parishioners over a period of eight years.  The new church was built by the side of the old tower in nine months.  In 1874, with money donated by Earl Cowper and Abel Smith Esq., the new tower and spire were added.

(Below)   The Baptist Church on the Cowbridge/Port Hill corner dates from the beginning of this century.  An earlier church remains on the far side of the present building, and is used as a church hall.

*(Right)    This is the Congregational Church in Cowbridge, built in the late 18th century, enlarged in 1844, and replaced by the present building in 1862.*

*(Below)    This is the Congregational Church built in 1862, now the United Refored Church. On the far side is the Church Hall.*

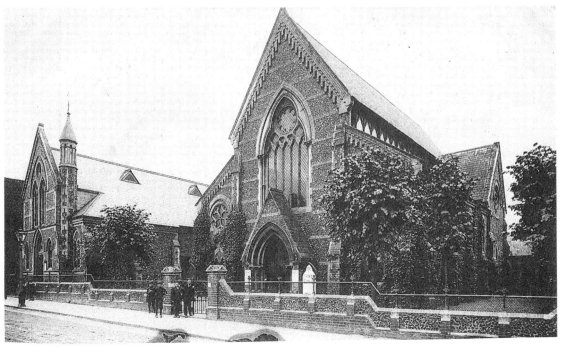

*(Above) Hale's Grammar School was founded in 1617 by Richard Hale. About 1900 it came under the control of the County Council and was known as Hertford Grammar School. It remained in use as H.G.S. until 1930, other buildings having been added to the original. In 1930 the school moved to new buildings — illustrated on page 60 — and later the name Richard Hale was revived.*

# Going to School

For the great majority of children, education was first provided by the churches. Early in the nineteenth century, National Schools supported by the Church of England and British Schools supported by the Non-conformist churches were opened. However, over the years the State has become almost completely responsible for education, acting through local education authorities.

*(Opposite, top)  This shows the original grammar school as one long room where all the classes in the school were taught.  A portrait of Richard Hale may be seen over the door.  In 1931 on the implementation of the Hadow Report in Hertford,  the buildings housed Longmore Senior Mixed School.*

*(Bottom)  Members of the Hertford Grammar School O.T.C. in 1935 with Major Moxom and Sergeant-Major Inman.*

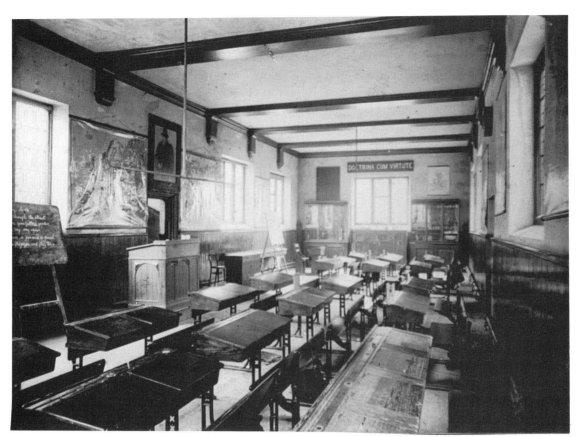

*(Above) The Green Coat School was one of nine provided for by Gabriel Newton of Leicester. Its first 'home' is not known but it moved into this building opposite All Saints' Church in 1812. In 1868, the school outgrew this building and moved. This is now a private residence.*

*(Below) The Green Coat School moved to this building in London Road (now Old London Road) in 1868. The school closed in 1894, the building was used for various educational purposes, then sold to Neale's Garage. It has recently been demolished. Gabriel Newton's beneficence continues in the Newton Exhibition Foundation, an educational charity.*

*(Above)    The Cowper Testimonial School, opened in 1841, was built to commemorate the generosity of Henry Cowper of Tewin Water whose greatest gift was the money to build and equip the Infirmary (now Hertford County Hospital). The school was a National School for 200 boys and 100 girls; it remained in use as a boys' school until 1957. The dual carriageway of London Road now passes over the site of the school.*

*(Below)  These boys were in the top class at the Cowper School just before it closed in 1957.  Some of them went to the new school in Balls Park, others left school.   The teacher is Len Green.*

*(Above)  By the late 1850's the Cowper School was overcrowded and this building, the Abel Smith Memorial School, was opened in 1861 to take all the girls; it was later known as All Saints' Girls' School. In 1931 it became a junior mixed school. The building is now used for a nursery school.*

*(Below)  This building, opened in 1850, housed the School of Industry for Girls which had opened in other premises in 1793. Apart from giving a basic education, its purpose was to prepare girls for service in the many large houses in the area. It appears to have been very successful in an age when "going into service" was the main work opportunity for girls.*

*(Right) All Saints' Infants' School was built in 1845 close by the church. The School of Industry premises were acquired in 1902 and this picture shows the two joined. It was later known as Faudel Phillips Infants' School. Only the School of Industry building now remains as part of the new Abel Smith School.*

*(Below)    The reception class at All Saints' Infants' School in 1913;    the teacher was Miss Lyons.*

*(Above)  Ragged schools provided education for children whose parents were too poor to pay the weekly pence asked at other schools. This one on Butcherley Green was opend in 1859, built with money from William Pollard, a Quaker who kept a draper's shop (now Graveson's). After the school closed in 1877, it served as a Mission Hall, then a Salvation Army Citadel, before its demolition.*

*(Opposite, top)  This building in Hertfordbury Road, was opened as St. Andrew's School in 1882. It became junior mixed in 1931, and moved to the Sele Farm estate well before the road became dual carriageway. In its new position it is the only remaining C. of E. school in the town.*

*(Bottom)  A class at St. Andrew's School in the late 1920's.*

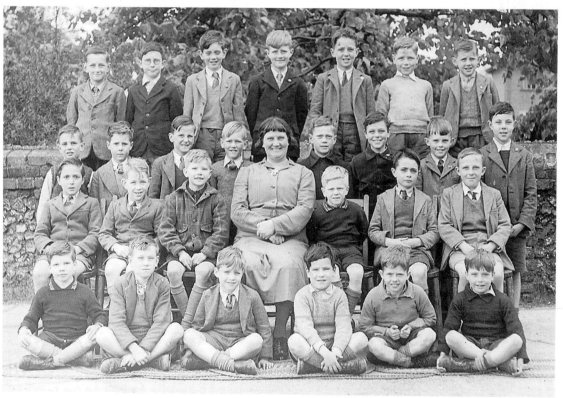

*(Above)   Before the building of County Hall, the county education service was administered from the building at 28 Castle Street.   This is a picture of the staff in 1932.*

*(Opposite, top)   This building in Dimsdale Street, behind the United Reformed Church, was a British School opened in 1863.   It became a junior mixed school in 1931, but was vacated early in the Second World War.   Afterwards, it became a handicraft centre for local schools, and closed in 1968.*

*(Bottom)   A group of pupils at Bengeo Junior Boys' School, photographed in 1946 with their teacher, Miss Cadd.   This school and the girls' school next door have now been replaced by a mixed school on another site, while the old sites have flats on them.*

*(Above)   A number of private schools have been part of the educational provision in the town.  St. Joseph's Convent School moved in 1952 from St. John's Street to a large house in Hertingfordbury. These girls moved with the Convent School.*

*(Below)   Haileybury College began as the East India College in Hertford Castle and moved to Hertford Heath in 1809.  The domed chapel was added in 1876.*

Haileybury College, Hertford                                    E. Munnings, Hertford.

*(Above)   Christ's Hospital, originally a City of London charity school, had premises in Hertford for centuries.  At first the Hertford school was largely for boys who lived in the cottages seen here.*

*(Below)   In 1906, Christ's Hospital at Hertford became a girls' school, the boys having gone to Horsham in Sussex. This shows the new dormitory blocks with some of the girls assembling by them. The girls also went to Horsham in 1984, since when the site has been developed for housing and commercial purposes.*

*The Golden Jubilee of Queen Victoria was celebrated in 1887. This is part of the procession which started in Ware Road and passed through the town.*

## Notable Occasions

We all welcome those occasions when the normal run of life is interrupted by unusual happenings. They may be anniversaries, the arrival of special visitors, civic celebrations, even an unusual sight in the street will give us the variety in life we need. This chapter includes a few of these notable occasions in the life of Hertford over the past hundred years or so.

*(Opposite, top)  This floral arch at the entry to Fore Street from Parliament Square was erected for the visit of the Prince of Wales (later Edward VII) in 1874.*

*(Bottom)  This picture of the hustings in Plough Meadow recalls the time before 1872, when all voting was in public, giving rise to bribery and corruption. The Ballot Act of that year introduced the secret ballot.*

*Sir George Faudel Phillips of Balls Park was Lord Mayor of London in 1897 when Queen Victoria's Diamond Jubilee was celebrated. He was given the Freedom of the Borough and an oak tree was planted at Old Cross to commemorate the event. Various reasons have been given for its failure to thrive, from disturbance by a circus elephant to a gas leak. Perhaps it was just not a good place to plant an oak tree. There is another view of the ill-fated oak on page 117.*

*Troops returning from the South African War in 1903 marched through the town with bayonets fixed, after their arrival at Cowbridge Station. A service of thanksgiving was held at Hartham for the safe return of men who had served in South Africa. More than a hundred men from the town were accepted for service after volunteering, only three of them died on service.*

*(Above)* In 1906, the Prince and Princess of Wales, later King George V and Queen Mary, came to Hertford to open the new accommodation for girls at Christ's Hospital. They are seen leaving Cowbridge Station.

*(Below)* Another view of the Prince and Princess of Wales on their way to Christ's Hospital.

*(Above)   A 1913 picture of the judge driving from his lodgings to preside at the Assizes at Shire Hall.  In later years he was taken by car but, since the establishment of Crown Courts, the Shire Hall houses only the magistrates' courts.*

*(Below)   On October 1st 1925, the York Herald presented to the Mayor, Alderman Josiah Wren, the Standard of Honor; the Borough had been designated an "Honor" in 1304 and in subsequent royal grants.  All the school children of the town attended the ceremony.  The original standard became fragile and a new one was dedicated in All Saints' Church on May 17th 1987.*

*(Above)   A gathering in the late 1940's not possible today:  local farmer Tim Muxworthy leading the Enfield Chase Hunt through Fore Street into Parliament Square.*

*(Below) In 673 A.D. the first synod of the English Church was held in Hertford. In 1973, the 1300th anniversary was celebrated, and senior churchmen led the procession from All Saints' Church to a ceremony in the Castle grounds.   At the rear are Lord Runcie, then Bishop of St. Albans, and Cardinal Heenan, Archbishop of Westminster.*

*(Above) The Synod celebrations were attended by the Queen Mother whose car is seen here being escorted to the Castle grounds.*

*(Below) The original synod is commemorated by stones in the Castle grounds and near the Roman Catholic Church. This metal statuary representing the five bishops attending was put on the side of the Castle Hall after the 1973 celebration.*

*(Above)  Canon Woolmore Wigram, Rector of St. Andrew's 1876-1897, is seen here with members of the St. Andrew's Cycle Club.  Their names from left to right are:  the Rev. Cockerton, Sidney Wickham, Mr. Walker, S. Durrant, Mr. Harvey, Douglas Garratt and E. Ilott.  The dog is unnamed.*

# Sports, Pastimes and Entertainment

How did townspeople use their leisure before the days of cinemas, radio and television?  There was much less leisure than there is today, but they seemed to use it well.  The rivers and the open spaces such as Hartham encouraged outdoor activities.  There were many sports clubs and the events at the Whit-Monday sports showed an interest in athletics and cycling.  And gardening was a popular pastime.

Circuses visited the town frequently, with impressive parades through the streets, causing truancy among schoolboys.  The Cold Bath (see page 97) had its own theatre and other inns had rooms where visiting players could perform.  A Mr. Lupino had a concert room at the east end of the town.  Among the entertainers recorded as visiting the town were Tomb Thumb, a band of "Ethiopian Serenaders" and the Infant Thalia who sang songs and gave impressions.  In 1845, Richardson's Rock Band came to Hertford before setting out on a tour of Paris and Vienna — it should be noted that "rock" did not mean what it does today: they simply played on stones.  In addition to these professionals, there were  amateur societies giving worthy performances, as there still are today, to the pleasure of their audiences.

*(Opposite, top)   Hertford Athletic Football Club, winners of the Hertford and District Junior League in the 1928-29 season.  Sitting in the centre are Alderman Josiah Wren and Cyril Stalley, headmaster of the Cowper School.*

*(Bottom)   The Bengeo Football Club team for the year 1958-59.*

BENGEO F.C. 1958-9

*(Above) Hertford Cricket Team in 1889: it appears that a hat of some kind was demanded for the occasion.*

*(Below)   A less formal cricket team at Balls Park in 1926.*

*(Above)   Hertford Brewery's cricket team of 1938 pictured in front of their pavilion.*

*(Below)   In 1963, Bengeo Cricket Club beat Hertford in the final of the George Fuller Cup.  The three members of the Bengeo team are, left to right, Rae Costin, Dennis Costin and Charles Toghill.*

For those who prefer to take their physical exercise at a slower speed gardening is ideal. Bengeo Cottage Gardeners is a society which continues to thrive and to produce an excellent annual show. This is part of the 1950 show.

(Opposite, top and bottom)  A circus parade in Ware Road about 1917, continuing the practice of showing itself to the town to attract customers. The large number of boys following the elephants suggests some gaps in the classrooms that day.

# Hertford's cinemas

*(Above) Hertford's first cinema was the People's Electric Theatre, which opened in November 1910. It seated 160 and there was also standing room. It closed in September 1914; Hines, jewellers, is now on its site in Maidenhead Street.*

*(Below) The Premier Cinema opened in Market Street on Christmas Eve 1910 with 220 seats; a small orchestra accompanied the films, and variety acts were introduced into programmes. In the 1920's it stopped showing films and became a theatre of varieties until 1929. In 1932 it opened as the Regent Cinema equipped to show "talkies". It finally closed in May 1943, the hairdressers "Jangles" occupies the site.*

*(Above)  The Castle Cinema opened in August 1914 reputedly with 1000 seats ranging in price from 3d. to 2s. and offering free storage of bicycles for patrons arriving by this means.  An orchestra accompanied the films.  It was modernised in 1939 with seating for 600, and after damage by the flying bomb of 1944 was repaired and re-opened in 1946.  It closed in 1959 and Castle Hall is now on the site.*

*(Below)  The County Cinema was opened in July 1933, far grander than the other two cinemas in the town, having its own car park, a café, 580 seats in the stalls and 578 in the balcony.  It was successful until television caused a decline in cinema-going.  Various plans to modify it for entertainment purposes came to nothing and it closed in October 1982.  An office block now stands on the site in Ware Road.*

*(Above) It was in front of Lombard House, the Hertford Club, that four prominent townsmen were killed on October 13th 1915. Mr. Jevons, the Borough Surveyor, Mr. Gregory, organist at All Saints', a draper Mr. Cartledge and Mr. Jolly, who worked in a local bank, all came out to look at a Zeppelin flying ship caught in the searchlights, when a stick of bombs was dropped on the town. Two soldiers were also killed in North Road.*

# In Time of War

For those actively involved, the First World War was a time when the horrible realities of all-out warfare were realised. From the start, the Second World War was accepted as an evil necessity in we were all involved. While Hertford was spared serious bombing, we remember many things which cannot be put into pictures — the shortages and strict rationing, which continued until 1951, the black-out and the drabness of everyday life and, for those who experienced life in the services, the long periods of boredom, interspersed with times of feverish activity. But we remember with pleasure our weekly ration of Tommy Handley and ITMA ("It's That Man Again!") and, above all, the unity of purpose which we have never achieved since.

*(Opposite, top) This Christmas card was sent by the Vicar of All Saints' Church to a serving soldier in 1917.*

*(Bottom) Victory in the First World War was celebrated by a ceremony in Fore Street in 1919. Cadets from Haileybury College and Hertford Grammar School paraded and fired a feu de joie.*

YOUR KING AND COUNTRY THANK YOU.   HOME WORDS No. 168

*All Saints', Hertford, remembers all of you this Christmas.*

Damage caused in a country town by a German raider. Below: Rear view of houses demolished showing also the bomb crater.

*(Opposite page, top)* In 1940, when Second World War air-raids began, a German land mine did damage to many houses in the Tamworth Road/Ware Road area. As far as is known, there were no deaths directly due to this incident. This is photograph is from a London newspaper and, for security reasons, the location is given simply as "a country town".

*(Opposite page, bottom)* On July 2nd 1944, a V2 flying bomb struck Mill Bridge. On the left was Ilott's shop attached to the Town Mill, next to Nicholls' fruit, flower and vegetable shop; to the right of this was Rush's leather goods shop.

*(This page)* The Flying bomb damage—back view. Mr. Nicholls is seen viewing the damage; this area is now covered by the lawn beside Castle Hall. On the other side of the river is the wreckage of what was the Brewery Tap, which had been attached to Wickham's Brewery until purchased by Wells and Winch, whose sign can be seen. This site remains derelict, part of the railings seen still stands. Across the road, Oliver's next to the Woolpack has a tarpaulin covering roof damage.

*(Above)  War brings shortages, especially of imported goods. These men in Bengeo were ensuring that they could continue to smoke by growing their tobacco — a picture taken in 1941.*

*(Below)  Victory in Europe - VE Day - was celebrated by children in Bengeo in May 1945.*

*Bengeo Estate VE Children's Party*

MAY, 1945

In commemoration of the Victory in Europe, 1945,

*A Celebration Party for Children*

was held in the Rectory Field, Bengeo.

*Rosemary Groom*

was a member of the Happy Party.

GOD SAVE THE KING

*One of Hertford's characters of the past, photographed by Elsden. It is entitled "Mardell, road minder, Hertingfordbury Road" though he may have been more of a road-mender than minder.*

# Hertford People

For a town of its size, Hertford has had a remarkable number of famous citizens, a few of whom are mentioned on these pages. There were others, from the important people who lived here during the Middle Ages (and others who were imprisoned in the Castle) to modern celebrities such as Eric Heffer, the former choirboy at Christ Church, Port Vale (where he organised a choirboys' strike) who became a noted left-wing Labour Member of Parliament.

*This plaque is on the building now occupied by Barclays Bank in Fore Street. After taking his degree at Emmanuel College, Cambridge, Samuel was ordained priest in the Church of England in 1626. He lost his living for nonconformity and in 1633 he went with Thomas Hooker, a leading nonconformist, to Boston, Massachusetts, taking his wife and family with him. In 1636 they moved with their congregation to Connecticut, where they established the town of Hartford. When Hooker died in 1647, Stone succeeded him as Pastor, a position he held until his death until 1663.*

*Thomas Dimsdale was a doctor who was one of the leaders in the use of inoculation to prevent serious forms of smallpox. He treated patients at Port Hill house, and it is believed he obtained his material for inoculation from the sufferers in the nearby Pest House. In 1768, at the request of Catherine the Great, he went to Russia and inoculated her and other members of the Tsarist Royal Family. The success of this mission resulted in his being made a Baron by Catherine, as well as being given valuable gifts. He made another visit in 1781 to treat other members of the Royal Family and for a while was Member of Parliament for Hertford. In 1798, Jenner introduced vaccination, a less dangerous treatment which used a modified virus discovered among those who had been in contact with cows.*

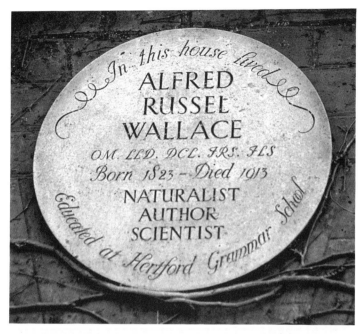

Alfred Russel Wallace came to Hertford with his family when he was about six years old, his mother having family connections here. The plaque is on the first of four houses they occupied in the town, now part of a group surgery in St. Andrew Street. In his book, My Life, he wrote of his pleasurable memories of Hartham and the Warren and in watching the production of oil and oilcake from linseed at Hornsmill. He went to Hertford Grammar School until he was 14, then helped his elder brother in land surveying. His encounter with Henry Walter Bates, an entomologist, started him on his work as a naturalist. He spent four years from 1848-52 in the Amazon Valley, partly with Bates, then a further eight years from 1854-62 in South-east Asia. On his return, he was in touch with Darwin, Huxley and other leading scientists of the day and he wrote a number of books. He arrived independently at the same conclusion as Darwin on "Natural Selection". His name is remembered on maps of the world showing animal distribution: "Wallace's Line", which follows a deep sea channel in the Pacific, separates the occurrence of Oriental mammals from those of Australasia.

*W.E. Johns was born on February 5th 1893 and, while he was still young, the family moved into 41 Cowbridge where his father carried on business as a tailor. After education at Hertford Grammar School, he went to work at Swaffham where he joined the Territorial Army in 1913. He was in the First World War from the beginning and took part in the disastrous Gallipoli campaign in 1915. He was accepted for the Royal Flying Corps in 1917 and in September 1918 he was shot down and taken prisoner. The picture shows him as a P.O.W. at Karlsruhe. After post war serve as a Recruiting Office for the R.A.F., he started writing on aviation and it was in 1932 that Captain James Bigglesworth, or "Biggles" was created. Since then he has been the idol of readers in many parts of the world.*

*(Above)   The Borough Council of 1907 in front of the Castle, the Mayor being Alderman William Graveson. The Borough Surveyor, Mr Jevons, wearing a bowler hat, was one of the four men killed outside the Hertford Club by a bomb from a Zeppelin in 1915.*

*(Below)   The members of Hertford Borough First Aid Post in the Second World War. The picture was taken in 1942 when they were the winning team in a county competition. The three in the centre are Mrs. H. Norris, Sister I.P. Chapman and Dr. G.W. May.*

This is the forerunner of McMullen's "Twenty-five Year Club" — it shows those who in 1968 had completed 30 years or more service to the brewery firm, totalling an amazing 900 years in all. The then chairman, Colonel Peter McMullen, is seated third from the right.

Long-serving members of the staff of Addis's — photographed in 1959, with Mr. Robert Addis Senior in the centre of the picture.

# Index

Abel Smith family   69, 126
Abel Smith School   132, 133
Adams, James   13
Addis Ltd   102-105, 166
All Saints' Church   48, 50, 52, 60,
  62, 122, 130, 145, 146, 156
All Saints' Girls' School   132
All Saints' Infants' School   133
Andrews, builders   74, 106
Austen, Jane   73

Back Street   26
Baker Street   54
Balfour, A.J., M.P.   24
Balfour Street   36
Ball, Bill   94
Balls Park   68, 69, 131, 142, 150
Baptist Church   41, 126
Barnardo's, Dr.   69
Bates Brothers,   116
Beane, River   34, 74
Beane Road   34, 80, 87
Beard's men's outfitter   11
Beckwith's antiques   41, 116
Bell Inn   97
Bengeo   39, 79, 123, 160
Bengeo Cottage Gardeners   152
Bengeo Cricket Club   151
Bengeo Football Club   148
Bengeo Junior Boys' School   137
Bengeo Street   40
"Biggles"   164
Bircherley Green ("Butcherley
  Green")  26, 28, 31, 32, 62, 134
Black Swan Inn   58
Blackbirds Inn   16
Boston, Mass., U.S.A.   162
Briant's Bell Foundry   17
Brickenden Bury   16, 73
British School   137
Bull Inn   28
Byde Street   37, 39, 110

Cadd, Miss   137
Camps Hill   45, 106
Cartledge, Mr. draper   156
Castle   8, 20, 21, 66, 138, 147, 165
Castle Cinema   18, 155
Castle Gates   18, 19
Castle Hall  18,23,83,91,147,155,159
Castle Street  16,21,55,58,60,137
Catherine the Great   162
Cawthorne   43, 57
Caxton Hill   100, 101
Cecil, Evelyn, M.P.   13
celluloid  102
Ceres statue   13
Chapman, Sister I.P.   165

Chequer Inn   14
Chequer Yard   66
cholera   62
Christ Church (Port Vale)   36, 161
Christ's Hospital   41, 54, 56, 61, 84,
  88, 138, 139, 144
Church Street   50, 60
cinemas   154, 155
Cockbush Avenue   52
Cold Bath Inn   97, 148
Congregational Church (United
  Reformed Church)  35, 127
Cordwainers' Street   26
Corn Exchange   8, 11, 13, 99
Costin, Dennis & Rae   151
County Cinema   155
County Hall   48, 56, 73, 134
County Hospital   45
Cowbridge   34, 35, 99, 126,
  127, 164
Cowbridge Station 34, 46, 84, 86,
  87, 119, 144
Cowper, Earl   23, 71, 126
Cowper, Henry   131
Cowper Testimonial School   48,
  131, 132
Cromwell, Oliver   52
Cromwell Road   52
Cross Keys Inn   99
Cross Lane   41, 44, 97
cycling   8, 30, 48, 115, 148

Darwin, Charles   163
Desborough, Lord   70, 71
Dicker Mill   74, 79
Dimsdale Arms   97
Dimsdale, Thomas (Baron)   35
Dimsdale Street   34, 99, 137
Dolphin Yard   66
Domesday Book   79, 80, 82, 83
Duncombe Arms   97
Duncombe Road   40
Duncombe, Tom   97
Durrant, Mr. S.   148
Dye family, chimney sweeps   108

Earl Haig pub   33
Ebenezer Baptist Chapel   41, 97
Edward VII, King   140
Ekins & Co   45, 106
Elizabeth, the Queen Mother   147
Elliott's music shop   56
Elsden "photographists"   121, 161
Epcombs   73

Fanshawe Street   39
Farquhar Street   39
Faudel Phillips Infants' School.  133
Faudel Phillips, Sir George  68, 142
Field and Marks   114
Fire Service   103

First Aid Post   165
flying bombs   155, 159
Folly Island   62, 74
Fordham, James, miller   77
Fore Street  8,16,17,26,33,48, 50,
  99,101,114,116  140,146,156,162
Friends' Meeting House   65, 122

Gaol, Hertford   84, 103
Garratt family   80, 148
Gascoyne Way  7,2,141,46,48,55,
  56,58,60
George V, King   144
Gilbertson and Page   116
Gladstone Arms   58
Goldings   69, 109
Graveson family   113 ,165
Graveson's store   30, 113, 134
Greaves's grocers   30
Green Coat School   130
Green Dragon Inn   19, 27
Green Street   28, 31, 65, 108

Hagsdell Road   48
Haileybury College   100, 138, 156
Hale Road   56, 60
Hale's cycles   48, 119
Hale's Grammar School   61, 128
Handley, Tommy   156
Harrison, Victor   100
Hartfield, Ken   101
Hartford, Conn. U.S.A.   41, 162
Hartham   88, 143, 163
Hartham Chapel   34
Hartham Lane   34, 86, 91, 93
Hayden's Court   65
Heenan, Cardinal   146
Heffer, Eric, M.P.   161
Hertford Athletic F.C.   148
Hertford Brewery cricket XI 151
Hertford County Hospital   131
Hertford Cricket Team   150
Hertford Grammar School  60,128,
  156, 163, 164
Hertfordshire County Council 69,73
Hertfordshire Mercury 16,100, 101
Hertingfordbury   47, 138
Hertingfordbury Road   41, 43,
  97, 134, 161
Highland Chief Inn   28
Holy Trinity Church   123
Honey Lane   26, 27, 28
Hooker, Thomas   162
Hope Brewery   91, 93
Hornsmill   82, 163

Ilott family   83, 148, 159
Inman, Sergeant-Major   128
insanitary housing   26, 34, 62

Jevons, Mr, Surveyor   156, 165

Jewson's, builders' merchants   74
Johns, Captain W.E.   164
Johnson family, butchers  119, 120

King's Head Hotel,   97

Lea, River   62, 74, 77, 80
Leahoe   73
Lee Navigation   62, 74, 77
Library   24, 25
Lion's Head Inn   32
Lombard House   28, 74, 156
London Road   48, 52, 61, 119,
   130, 131
Longmore School   61, 128
Longmore's, solicitors   21
Lupino's Concert Room   148
Lyons, Miss   133

Maidenhead Inn   27, 65
Maidenhead Street   26, 27, 28,
   41, 66, 101, 113, 115, 122, 154
Maidenhead Yard   65
Mangrove Road   48
Mardell, road minder,   161
markets   9, 26, 31, 32, 119
Market Street   11, 13, 31, 116, 154
Marshall, R.L.   101
Mary, Queen   144
May, Dr. G.W.   165
Mayflower Place   47
McMullen and Son  24, 86, 87, 91,
   93, 94, 166
McMullen, Colonel Peter   166
McMullen, Osmond Henry   19
Methodist Church   52
Militia Barracks   103
Mill Bridge  23, 91, 93, 110, 121, 159
Mimram, River   71, 74
Mission Hall,   134
Molewood Mill   34, 79
Molewood Road   34, 80
Morris, William   69
Moxom, Major   128
Munnings' china shop   110
Muxworthy, Tim   146

Neale's furnishing store   110
Neale's garage   50, 61
Nelson Street,   80
Newbridge Inn   99
Newton, Gabriel   130
Nicholls Brewery   36, 91
Norris, Mrs. H.   165
North Road  41, 44, 45, 46, 84-87,
   97, 121, 156

Old Coffee House   26, 28
Old Cross   18, 25, 34, 116, 142
Old Mill Stream pub   37
Oliver's shop   159

Panshanger   23, 70, 71
Paradise Court,   66
Parliament Square   8, 19, 114, 146
Pateman family   115
Pearson, Sir Alfred   73
Pearson, Sir Edward   16
Pegs Lane   58
People's Electric Theatre,   154
Pest House   39, 162
Plough Field   61, 140
Plough Hotel   52, 61
Poet's Corner   66
Pollard family   113, 134
Poor Estate charity   14, 15
Port Hill   34, 38, 39, 126, 162
Port Vale   34, 36, 37, 80, 161
Post Office   8, 14, 15, 66
Premier Cinema   154
Prince Albert Cottages   35
Priory Mill   74, 79
Priory Wharf   74

Quakers   38, 113, 122, 134
Queen's Road   50, 56
Quelch and Brown's cycle   30

Ragged School   62, 122, 134
Railway Street   11, 26 , 31, 32, 33,
   65, 122
Ram Inn   9
Red Lion Inn   57
Regent Cinema   154
Reindeer public house   38
Repton, Humphrey   71
Rib, River   74, 77
Richard Hale School   60, 128
Robinson family   113
Roman Catholic Church   122, 147
Rooks Alley   48
Rowlandson, Thomas   97
Russia   162

Salisbury Arms.   97
Salisbury, Marquess of   19, 97
Salisbury Square   30, 113
Salvation Army   134
Sele Mill   34, 45, 80
Sele Road   43, 45, 106
Shire Hall   8, 11, 26, 50, 100, 145
Simon Balle School   68
Simpson's, printers   17
South African War   25, 143
South Street   33, 88
Sovereign House   60
Spencer Corner   114
St. Andrew Street   41, 43, 55,
   57, 66, 115, 116, 163,
St. Andrew's Church   44, 57, 122,
   126, 148
St. Andrew's School   134
St. Edmund's College   106

St. John's Church   122
St. John's Street   138
St. Joseph's Convent School   137
St. Leonard's Church   123
St. Mary the Less  Church 25, 122
St. Nicholas Church   41, 122
St. Nicholas Hall   41, 116
Stalley, Cyril   148
Steam Laundry,   102
Stephen Austin & Sons   100, 101
Stone, Samuel   162
synod of 673 A.D.   146

Tallow House   62
Tamworth Road.   116, 159
Taylor, Eric, cooper   93
Taylor's hardware shop.   116
Thistledoo Café   13
Toghill, Charles   151
tolls   18, 23
Tonwell   122
Town Mill   23, 83, 159
Townshend, Marquess   68
Traveller's Rest Inn   99
Two Brewers   36

United Reformed Church   35
University of Hertfordshire.   68

VE Day   160
Victoria, Queen   140, 142
Vine Inn   30

Wackett family   115
Walker, Mr.   148
Wallace, Alfred Russel   163
War Memorial   8, 16, 17
Ware Park   106
Ware Park Mill   77
Ware Road   52, 61, 100, 102,
   104, 119, 140, 152, 155, 159
Wash, The   18, 19, 115
Water Lane   58
Waterford   69
Water's Garage   121
Webb, William brewers  82, 91, 159
Welwyn Road   46
Wesley, John   122
West Street   46, 55, 58, 91
White Hart Inn   30
White Horse   47
Wickham, Sidney   148
Wickham's Brewery   91, 159
Wigram, Canon W.   148
Willson's wine shop   13
Wimblett, Harry D.   99
workhouse   52
Wren, Alderman Josiah   145, 148

Young's brewery,   88

Zeppelin   156, 165